SALES SUCCESS

SALES
SUCCESS

BRIAN TRACY

AMACOM AMERICAN MANAGEMENT ASSOCIATION
New York • Atlanta • Brussels • Chicago • Mexico City
San Francisco • Shanghai • Tokyo • Toronto • Washington, D.C.

Bulk discounts available. For details visit:
www.amacombooks.org/go/specialsales
Or contact special sales:
Phone: 800-250-5308 / E-mail: specialsls@amanet.org
View all the AMACOM titles at: www.amacombooks.org

Library of Congress Cataloging-in-Publication Data

Tracy, Brian.
Sales success / Brian Tracy.
    pages cm
Includes index.
ISBN 978-0-8144-4919-6 (hardcover) — ISBN 0-8144-4919-0 (hardcover) — ISBN 978-0-8144-4920-2 (ebook) 1. Selling. 2. Success in business. I. Title.
HF5438.25.T7136 2015
658.85—dc23

                                                               2014033825

About AMA

American Management Association (www.amanet.org) is a world leader in talent development, advancing the skills of individuals to drive business success. Our mission is to support the goals of individuals and organizations through a complete range of products and services, including classroom and virtual seminars, webcasts, webinars, podcasts, conferences, corporate and government solutions, business books, and research. AMA's approach to improving performance combines experiential learning—learning through doing—with opportunities for ongoing professional growth at every step of one's career journey.

Printing number
10 9 8 7 6 5 4 3 2 1

CONTENTS

Introduction

I HAVE BEEN in sales since I was 10 years old, when I began selling Rosamel beauty soap to earn my way to YMCA camp that summer. Ever since then, I have been studying, reading books, and trying to learn more about selling because I wanted to be successful at it, just as you do.

Early in my career, I began asking, "Why is it that some salespeople are more successful than others?"

Why is it that some salespeople earn more money, faster and easier, and make more sales? Why do they enjoy greater success, acquire better material benefits, such as cars, homes, and beautiful clothes, and achieve greater satisfaction from their careers while the great majority of salespeople underachieve and underperform?

The First Principle

Then I discovered the famous 80/20 rule known as the Pareto principle. This rule says that 80 percent of the sales are made by 20 percent of the salespeople. This means 20 percent of the sales are therefore made by 80 percent of the salespeople. When I learned this principle, I made a decision: I was going to do whatever I had to do to get into the top 20 percent. And I did.

Some years ago, a major insurance company with thousands of agents decided to test out the validity of the 80/20 rule in terms of its income and sales. The company subsequently ran all of its agents' sales and income data through a computer and found that this rule held true. Twenty percent of the agents were generating 80 percent of the business. Company managers then asked what this meant in terms of annual income. They found that the top 20 percent of the agents were earning, on average, sixteen times what the bottom 80 percent were earning. Did this means that the top 20 percent were sixteen times better, smarter, or more competent than those in the bottom 80 percent?

The answer is obvious: No one is sixteen times better or smarter than someone else. Some people are just a little better in certain ways, consistently, over time.

The Top 20 Percent of the Top 20 Percent

They also looked at the top 4 percent of their agents (the top 20 percent of the top 20 percent) and compared their earnings to agents in the bottom 80 percent of sales and income. It turned out that the top 4 percent of agents were earning, on average, thirty-two times that of those in the bottom 80 percent. Taking this one step further, they compared the top 0.8 percent of agents (the top 20 percent of the top 4 percent) and found that this elite group was making, on average, more than fifty times the income of the people in the bottom 80 percent.

In every city or large office there was one person, by himself, who was earning as much as (or more than) fifty full-time adults selling the same products to the same people at the same prices, under the same competitive conditions and out of the same office. When the average salesperson, especially in all-commission fields, is earning $30,000 to $40,000 per year, the top 10 percent in those fields earn more than $800,000 per year, and some of them earn in the millions.

Make a Decision

Because of this incredible disparity in sales and income, the aim of every salesperson in every field should be to join the top 20 percent in that industry. The top 20 percent always sell well and make an exceptional living, no matter what the current market conditions. They are always employed and always in demand, and they enjoy their work the most.

Why is it that there are such enormous disparities in sales performance? In *Sales Success*, I will share with you some of the answers that have been discovered.

Develop the Winning Edge

One of the most important discoveries in human performance in the twentieth century was that the top performers in every field, including the field of sales, are only a little bit better that their peers in certain critical areas.

This small difference in performance is called the "winning edge." The top people in each field have developed the winning edges in those fields, and, as a result, they achieve extraordinary performance and extraordinary results.

My favorite analogy is that of a horse race. In a horse race, the horse that comes in first, by a nose, wins ten times the prize money of the horse that comes in second, by a nose. Is the horse that comes in first by a nose ten times better or faster than the horse that comes in second? Is the horse that wins 10 percent faster than the horse that loses? And the answer is no. The horse that wins is only a nose faster. In a photo finish, this can be as little as three inches.

The salesperson that closes the sale for his or her company gets 100 percent of the business and 100 percent of the commission. Is the salesperson who gets the sale twice as good as the salesperson who did not make the sale? In every case, the differences between the highest performers and the lowest performers are very small, marginal edges in skill and ability.

The person who earns $250,000 a year in sales is not ten times smarter or better, or working ten times harder than the person who earns $25,000 per year, selling the same product.

Intelligence Is Not the Key

In a study in New York some years ago, researchers selected 1,000 adults at random and measured their IQs. They found that the difference between the person with the highest IQ and the person with the lowest IQ was two and a half times. But the person earning the most in this group—which was not necessarily the person with the highest IQ—was earning more than 100 times more than the lowest earner in this sample group. The conclusion is simple: It is not raw talent or ability that accounts for great success. Everyone has natural sales talents and abilities. Your success is determined solely by what you do with those natural talents and abilities.

The Magic Touch

Top salespeople have been analyzed extensively to find out how they think and behave. What emerges from these studies is the finding that the highest-paid salespeople have an easy ability to enter into friendly relationships with a great number of diverse prospects and customers. They establish rapport early and build high levels of trust in the course of the sales process. In fact, personality factors probably account for 80 percent or more of sales success.

Interpersonal effectiveness is based, more than any other factor, on the self-image and self-esteem of the salesperson. There seems to be a direct relationship between self-esteem and sales success. Salespeople who like and respect themselves tend to like and respect their customers. In turn, their customers tend to like and respect them, and are willing to follow their product or service recommendations.

The Winning Feeling

Psychologists use a term "performance-based self-esteem" to explain this relationship between self-esteem and personal performance. The conclusion is simple: The more you like yourself, the better you do your work; the better you do your work, the more you like yourself. Each feeds off the other. The better you get, the better you get. The more successful you are, the more you feel like a "winner." The more you enjoy this winning feeling, the harder you work, the more people you see, and the better sales results you get.

In the pages that follow, I will give you a series of specific methods, techniques, and strategies that you can use to dramatically improve your performance. This improvement in your performance will naturally cause you to like and respect yourself even more, which will then lead to even higher levels of performance. You will get onto an upward spiral of success and personal power that will propel you to the top of your field. Let's begin.

ONE

Become Brilliant on the Basics

WHEN VINCE LOMBARDI was brought in from the New York Giants to take over the Green Bay Packers in Wisconsin, the team had been performing poorly for several years.

When he was asked what he was going to change or do differently to move his team into championship contention, he said these famous words, "We are not going to try anything fancy; we are just going to become the best team in the National Football League at kicking, running, passing, and catching. We're going to become brilliant on the basics."

He went on to say, "We are going to run each play so smoothly and efficiently that, even if the other team knows what we are doing, they will be unable to stop us."

High-performing salespeople are those who have, first of all, identified the basics of sales success, and, second, have become brilliant on those basics.

The Basics of Sales Success

There are seven key results areas that determine sales effectiveness. Give yourself a grade from one (low) to ten (high) in each of these seven areas (listed below). Remember that a weakness in any one area can be enough to hold you back from realizing your full potential in sales.

In fact, your weakest key skill largely determines the height of your sales and the size of your income. Sometimes, just bringing yourself up in your weakest key skill area can lead to a dramatic increase in your sales results.

Here are the "big seven":

1. *Prospecting.* Find and spend time with more and better prospects.

2. *Building Rapport and Trust.* Take the time to understand and empathize with the prospect so that he likes you, trusts you, and is willing to discuss his needs and problems with you.

3. *Identifying Needs.* Ask well-formulated and structured questions to uncover the real problems, wants, and needs of your prospect as it relates to what you sell.

4. *Presenting.* Move from the general to the particular and show your qualified prospects that your

product or service is the best choice for them at this time, all things considered.

5. *Answering Objections.* Present logical and conclusive answers for the natural objections that most prospects have regarding the price and capabilities of your product.

6. *Closing the Sale and Asking for Action.* Bring the sales conversation to a satisfactory conclusion with a closed sale and a signed order or contract.

7. *Getting Resales and Referrals.* Provide excellent follow-up customer service such that the customer is so happy that he buys again and recommends your products/services to his friends.

Total your score and divide it by seven to get your coefficient of sales effectiveness today. If your average score is less than five, your sales results are probably less than satisfactory. And the area where you scored the lowest is probably holding you back from sales success more than any other factor.

Old and New Models of Selling

Almost all top salespeople use what I call the "new model of selling." This is very different from the old model, which is still taught by many companies and used extensively by many salespeople. Each of the models, the new and the old, has four parts.

The first part of the old model, about 10 percent, begins with the approach—the first contact. The salesperson meets the prospect and says something like, "Hi, how are you?" before engaging in small talk about the latest football game or television program. The salesperson then launches straight into the sales conversation.

The second part of the old model involves quickly qualifying the prospect to determine whether the person is in a position to buy your product or service. Salespeople have been taught supposedly clever qualifying questions to make sure that the prospect could both use and afford the product before wasting any time on a sales presentation.The third part of the old model is presenting your product or service in the best light possible by showing prospects what the product consists of and then trying to get them to buy it. The salesperson was taught to talk as much about the benefits as possible, and then to answer objections with a series of clever questions and answers.

The final part of the old model of selling—fully 40 percent of the sales process—is closing the sale. The general assumption was that all of sales effectiveness comes down to the ability of the salesperson to close the sale using a variety of techniques.

New Customers, New Methods

Today, the old way of selling does not work at all. Customers have changed completely in their knowledge and sophistication, and successful salespeople, those in the top 20 percent, have learned to sell to customers the way that customers want to be sold to.

The new model of selling is like an inverted pyramid, with the bulk of the pyramid at the top and the point at the bottom. The pyramid is divided into four parts. The first part, 40 percent of the sales conversation, is simply to build trust. Trust is the most important single factor in determining the purchasing decision, and in all relationships between people, for almost all reasons.

The second part of the new model, 30 percent, is to identify needs accurately. Take your time to ask a series of prepared and structured questions that allow you to fully understand the customer's situation before you even mention or discuss your product or service.

The next 20 percent of the new model is for you to present your product or service, based on what the customer has said, and show your customer how your product or service can satisfy the needs that have been clearly identified in your conversation with the customer up to this point.

The final 10 percent of the new model of selling is to ask the customer to make a buying decision, to confirm that what you are offering is what the customer needs and wants, and to get the customer to take action today. The more time you take to build trust, the easier it is for you to make an effective presentation and to close or confirm the sale at the end.

Relationship Selling

This new model is based on what we call "relationship selling." The key to success in selling today is developing high-quality professional business relationships with customers.

This model requires building high levels of trust and credibility, identifying needs carefully and accurately, showing the customer that your product or service will satisfy those needs, and then encouraging your customer to take action and wrap up the transaction.

Throughout this book, we will be talking about relationship selling. We will return continually to these two concepts: 1) the importance of building credible relationships and 2) the importance of becoming brilliant on the basics. The starting point of your becoming the best in your field, and moving into the top 20 percent or even the top 10 percent in your business, is to identify the key skills necessary for sales excellence, and then determine what you have to do to become excellent in each of those areas.

ACTION EXERCISES

1. Give yourself a grade of one to ten in each of the seven key result areas, and determine where you are the strongest and where you are the weakest.

2. Select one key skill area where you are weak and begin working every day on becoming better in that area.

TWO

Stay Enthusiastic

THE 80/20 RULE applies to successful selling. Most of your success—fully 80 percent and maybe even more—will be determined by your attitude, your personality, and your level of motivation.

It has been said that the critical variable in a sales conversation is a "transfer of enthusiasm." The sale takes place when you transfer your enthusiasm and belief in the goodness and value of your product or service into the mind of the customer. Like an electrical connection, when the spark of enthusiasm passes from you to your customer, the sale is made.

Enthusiasm is the key to establishing good relationships with buyers and closing sales. You need to be enthusiastic about yourself, your product, and your company to be able to transfer enthusiasm to another person. This enthusiasm is something you develop, like physical fitness. No one is born with it naturally.

Keep Your Energy High

There are several techniques you can employ each day to develop and maintain high levels of enthusiasm and selling energy.

Have Positive Expectations

This is one of the greatest motivators of all. Your expectations determine your attitude. And your attitude determines how you treat other people, and how they respond to you.

You develop an attitude of positive expectations by always expecting to do well. Expect that each person you talk to is a potential prospect. Expect that people will like you and be open to your presentation. Believe in yourself and your ability to be a top performer in your field.

Use Positive Self-Talk

Talk to yourself in a positive way all the time. Fully 95 percent of your emotions are determined by how you talk to yourself on an ongoing basis. Successful people make a habit of deliberately filling their minds with positive statements that are consistent with the way they want to be perceived, and the goals they want to achieve.

Successful salespeople love their work. They believe in their product or service. They are committed to their companies and to their customers. As a result, they continually reinforce these commitments in their minds and resist negative experiences by repeating, *"I love my work! I love my work! I love my work!"*

Practice Positive Visualization

Feed your mind continually with clear mental pictures of the person you want to be, doing what you want to do. "What you see is what you get."

In sport, and in sales, the regular practice of the "mental rehearsal" is a powerful tool you can use to keep yourself positive and motivated, and performing at your best, all day long. In a mental rehearsal, you close your eyes and create a clear picture of yourself as the best person you can be, selling with the highest level of effectiveness that you can imagine. Each time you replay this picture in your mind, it is accepted as a command by your subconscious. When you go into the actual sales situation, your subconscious mind will give you the energy, enthusiasm, and positive attitude consistent with your mental picture. This technique can help you more than anything else to be successful.

Consume Positive Mental Food

You know that if you eat healthy, nutritious food, you will have more energy and will perform better throughout the day. In the same way, when you feed your mind with positive mental food—what we call mental protein—you will think with greater clarity and feel better about yourself all day long.

Here are three things that you can do to improve your mind, feel better about yourself, and move rapidly toward joining the top 20 percent in the sales field:

1. *Read for thirty to sixty minutes each day.* Reading is to the mind as exercise is to the body. Get the best sales books that you can and, for an hour each morning, read up on the best sales methodologies, strategies, and techniques ever developed. Read newsletters, articles, and magazines on selling.

2. *Listen to educational CDs and audio books.* In your car, use your smartphone to listen and learn as you drive to appointments. Turn your car into a "classroom on wheels." As Zig Ziglar said, "Enroll in automobile university and attend full-time for the rest of your career."

3. *Attend every seminar that you can.* Resolve today to attend four seminars each year, or about one every three months. Sit in the front row and take good notes. Talk to the instructor or speaker and ask questions. Take the time to meet the other people who are attending and ask them what they have learned that is most important.

When you return home from a seminar, review your notes completely—ideally, once a week for the first month. Think continually in terms of the specific actions that you can take to implement the ideas that you have just learned. Make the seminar a rich and rewarding experience for your career.

Get Around Positive People

The people you associate with have an inordinate effect on your thinking and on your emotions. For this reason, resolve to get around winners. Associate with positive people who are going somewhere in their careers. As Zig Ziglar said, "You cannot fly with the eagles if you continue to scratch with the turkeys."

One of my students told me how he went from the bottom to the top of his sales force. When he began as a junior salesman, he would hang out with the other junior salespeople, who spent most of their time in the office shuffling their business cards and talking about what they were going to do.

He noticed that the top salespeople were seldom in the office, and when they were, they were busy making calls and organizing presentations. So he did something that changed his life. He went up to one of the top salespeople and asked for advice on managing his time.

The top salesman, surprised at this request, because it was so rare, showed him how he managed his time each day. The new salesman did exactly what the top salesman was doing, and within a week he noticed that his sales activity and results were improving.

He then began asking the other top salespeople for advice on what programs to listen to, what to read, what to say in a sales conversation, and so on. In every case, the top salespeople were helpful. It was no surprise that within six months, he was also one of the top salespeople. He was now associating with the top people in his company. They got together on a regular basis to talk about different ways to improve their sales. Within a year he was one of the top salesmen in his company, and he never looked back.

Become an Expert in Your Field

Study your products and services carefully and read your brochures from cover to cover. Become so knowledgeable about what you sell that you could give a presentation from memory if you lost all your sales materials.

Study your business and industry. Study your competitors. Understand the products and services they sell, and how what you sell is different from and superior to their offerings. The better you know your products, services, competitors, and the market in general, the more confidence you will have and the more respected you will be by your customers.

Get Serious About Your Work

Remember that, as a professional salesperson, you are a member of a *profession*. When you rise to the top of your field, you can earn as much or more than a doctor, dentist, architect, or engineer—people with many years of university qualifications.

Professionals at the top of their fields invest a lot of time keeping current with what is going on in their industries. They take their work seriously. They resolve to excel—to be better than their competitors. They want to be known as the top people in their fields. Above all, professionals are committed to doing an excellent job in their work, and to continually improving, getting better and better every day and every week. So should you.

ACTION EXERCISES

1. Resolve today to engage in personal development as a lifelong practice. Begin acquiring books on sales and resolve to read one chapter each day, from now on, for the rest of your sales career.

2. Say these words: *I like myself and I love my work!* Repeat this sentence over and over again throughout the day, first thing in the morning, and whenever you have a disappointment or a setback.

THREE

Personal Management Skills: The Inner Game

TO GET INTO THE top 20 percent in your field, and then the top 10 percent, 5 percent, and even one percent—where the big money is—you have to have everything going for you. The world of sales today, in any field, with any product or service, is more competitive than it has ever been before, except for tomorrow and the next day, and the day after that. Your goal must be to win this competition.

My favorite word in describing success is *clarity*. In my estimation, clarity accounts for 95 percent of your success and achievement in anything that you attempt to do, in both your personal and your business life.

The number one reason why some people are more successful than others is because they are absolutely clear about who they are, what they want, and exactly what they have to do to get it. Clarity requires a tremendous amount of thinking and rethinking. As Thomas Edison said, "The hardest work in the world is thinking, which is why most people never do it."

Set Big Goals for Yourself

Begin by setting clear personal *income* goals for yourself on a monthly and annual basis. How much do you want to earn each month? How much do you want to earn each year? These are your targets. Everything you do must be aimed at hitting or exceeding these targets.

One of my sales students was already reasonably successful. Nonetheless, she set a goal to double her income in the next twelve months. She then began exploring all the things that she could do to sell and earn twice as much. One of her friends suggested that the simplest way would be for her to double the size of each sale that she was making.

That idea had never occurred to her. She began looking around to determine what kind of customers made larger purchases than the customers she was selling to at the moment did. Over the next year, she reoriented her entire sales process so that she was selling more, and more often, to bigger and better customers. By the end of the year, her average sale was double what it had been at the beginning of the year. She was still working the same number of hours and making the same number of sales, but each one was twice as large as the sales she had been making before.

Know Your Ratios

Once you have determined how much you want to sell and earn, you must then determine the exact sales activities that you will have to engage in to earn that amount.

Here is the great discovery: When and where you make individual sales is largely out of your control. But your actions are completely under your control. The good news is that, by controlling your sales activities, you indirectly control your sales results.

The three primary activities of sales success are: prospecting, presenting, and closing.

Begin by determining how many new prospects you will have to contact and talk to each day and each week to achieve your desired sales results. One of the first acts you engage in as a sales professional is to keep accurate records of the number of calls you make each day and each week.

Look at the number of presentations or face-to-face meetings that you set up as a result of your prospecting. For example, let us say that you have to call on twenty new people to get five face-to-face appointments. (This is not an unusual number in a competitive market.)

The next part of selling is following up and closing the sale and keeping track: Let us say that you have to make twenty initial calls to get five appointments, and you have to make five presentations to get two prospective customers for follow-up. From these two prospective customers you will get one sale, on average.

Now you know your *ratios*. They are 20:5:2:1. You have to make twenty calls on the front end to get one sale on the back end.

Now, calculate the average size of each of your sales and your average personal commission or earnings on each sale. With these numbers, you now have clear targets to aim at.

Your strategy going forward is to, first of all, keep your funnel full. Make sure that you continually feed your "sales system" with a steady stream of new prospects. Second of all, resolve to improve—to get better in each of the critical areas of prospecting, presenting, and closing the sale. Call on better prospects and sort them out faster. Make better and more effective presentations. Follow up and close more sales. Improve your ratios in each area.

Set Your Priorities

The essence of personal management really comes down to your ability to set priorities and to stick to them. Use the 80/20 rule. Remember that 80 percent of your results will come from 20 percent of your activities. Keep focusing on the most valuable use of your time.

If *clarity* is the first word in personal success, then *focus* is the second word. Resolve to become results-oriented as opposed to activity-oriented. Focus on the results you want to accomplish, and of those, the most important results.

Develop a sense of urgency and a bias for action. A sense of urgency is one of the rarest qualities in business, or in any field. Every top salesperson has a sense of urgency. Move quickly whenever you have an idea or see an opportunity. Sometimes a few minutes will make all the difference between a major sale and nothing at all.

Keep asking, "Why am I on the payroll?"

The truth is that you are on the payroll to make sales. Your job is to prospect, present, and close. It is to get sales results—morning, noon, and night. Continue to ask yourself the magic question: "Is what I am doing right now leading to a sale?"

If what you are doing right now is not leading to a sale, stop doing it immediately and start doing things that are sales-achieving rather than just tension-relieving. You are the president of your own Professional Sales Corporation.

You are in charge of your own career. You are responsible for everything that you are and everything that you accomplish. Avoid the trap of the low performer who talks a lot but actually does little.

ACTION EXERCISES

1. Resolve today to keep an accurate record of your sales activities. How many calls do you make each day? How many customers do you meet with each day? How many sales do you make each day or week? How much do you earn per sale?

2. Set priorities on your work, and always ask, "What is the most valuable use of my time right now?"

FOUR

Personal Management Skills: The Outer Game

THERE ARE A SERIES of habits, rituals, and activities practiced by the highest-paid salespeople in every field. One of the most important rules in life is that, if you do what the most successful people do, you will soon enjoy the results and rewards that the most successful people get.

In every field, the foundation skills for success begin with learning and practicing what the top people in that field do. This advice applies to sports, music, entertainment, and especially to sales and business. Once you have mastered the basics and are achieving high levels of personal and financial success, you can then begin improvising and developing your own methods and techniques. But learn and do what the top people do first.

Get Going Early

The first habit you should develop is to get up and get going early. A recent study of the highest-paid Americans shows that with few exceptions, they arise before six in the morning. They develop certain rituals that they follow each day, like exercising, meditating, reading something educational or inspirational, dressing to look great, planning their day on paper, and getting going at an early hour.

A good discipline is that you try to make your first meeting at 8:00 a.m. or earlier. Many top salespeople invite a busy prospective customer to meet them for breakfast at a restaurant or a café near the customer's office. Since very few people are ever invited out for breakfast, most people will accept the invitation. These sixty minutes together in the morning often set the stage for a long-term business relationship.

When Are You Working?

According to different studies that go back to 1928, the average salesperson works only about ninety minutes per day. The rest of the time is spent warming up, preparing, chatting with coworkers, checking e-mail, reading the paper, drinking coffee, and numerous other things. But by the end of the day, the average salesperson has only spent ninety minutes working.

Increase Your "Face Time"

You are only working when you are face-to-face with the prospective customer. We call this "face time." It is only when you are face-to-face with a prospective customer that you have an opportunity to make a sale. And since your work consists of making sales, when you are not in direct contact with customers, you are not working.

Do you want to double your income? It's simple. Double the number of minutes that you spend face-to-face with prospects and customers. Use your skills of time management and personal organization to spend more and more face time with people who can buy. If you double the amount of time you spend face-to-face with prospects and customers, by the law of averages, you will double your sales and double your income.

Sell More Stuff

Sometimes, I ask my sales audiences, "Why do you get up in the morning?"

After a little bit of thinking and mulling, they finally agree that the reason they get up in the morning and go to work is to make money.

I call it the "MMM theory of sales activity." The reason that you get up out of bed and go to work in the morning is so that you can make more money (MMM).

And how do you make more money in the world of sales or business? The answer is that you sell more stuff (SMS).

Your job is to "make more money" by "selling more stuff." By this definition, you are only working when you are selling more stuff. And what are the three ingredients of selling more stuff? They are "prospecting, presenting, and closing the sale.

"Therefore, by your own definition, you are only working when you are prospecting, presenting, and closing. You are only working when you are face-to-face with people who can and will buy and pay within a reasonable period of time. Anything else that you may be doing during the day is a relative waste of time. Do as little of it as possible.

Make Every Minute Count

Make every minute count. Top people in every field, including sales, think of their time in terms of minutes rather than hours or half hours. Unsuccessful people earning low incomes think of their time in terms of hours or days or even weeks.

Make every minute count, especially during "prime external time," when customers are available. Allocate your time in ten-minute increments. When you take control of your minutes, your hours will take care of themselves.

Concentrate Your Energies

If the first word for success in sales is *clarity*, and the second word is *focus*, the third word for success is *concentration*. Be absolutely clear about what you are trying to do, focus intently on that one thing, and concentrate single-mindedly on it until it is complete. With these three qualities developed as habits, you will accomplish more in the next year than many people accomplish in five or ten years.

Resist Distraction

Today, most people are suffering from the "attraction of distraction." They are so preoccupied with their smartphones, tablets, e-mail messages, and telephone calls that they are continually distracted from doing the hard, steady work of prospecting, presenting, and closing. They are constantly being thrown off their game by social media and other interruptions.

There is a simple formula for success in today's high-tech world: *Leave things off.* Or, better still, turn things off. Put your smartphone into silent mode. Don't check your e-mail in the morning. Then, check it only twice a day. Do not allow technology to control your life and ruin your future. Turn it on, use it as a communications tool, and then turn it off and leave it off.

Go the Extra Mile

Resolve to go the extra mile, every day. Always do more than is expected of you. Exceed even your own expectations. Resolve to work harder than your competition does, both inside your company and on the outside. There are never any traffic jams on the extra mile.

Make the "second effort," even when the sale seems lost. To paraphrase Vince Lombardi again, when you are tired and discouraged at the end of the day, make the second effort and try once more. Very often, making one last try, one more call, or asking one more question is what turns the whole sales situation around.

I learned as a young salesman that the best sales are always made at the end of the longest day, at the end of the longest street, with the last person on whom you call.

I have found this to be true, over and over again.

Guard Your Health

An important part of the outer game of success is guarding your health carefully. Eat the right foods—foods that give you strength and energy. Avoid the three white poisons: salt, sugar, and white flour products. All three of these substances rob you of energy and diminish your enthusiasm and your ability to sell effectively. Instead, eat high-protein foods that nourish your muscles and your brain and enable you to perform at a high level.

Look the Part

Take special care of your appearance. Make sure that you look excellent on the outside, like a winner in every respect. Fully 95 percent of the first impression that you make on other people will be determined by your clothes, because even on a warm day, your clothes cover 95 percent of your body. Your face, hair, and grooming are enormously important in projecting an image of confidence and credibility. Look around you at the highest-paid people in your industry and then dress and groom the way they do.

Be Physically Fit

You need about 200 minutes of exercise per week to be trim, fit, and healthy. This doesn't mean that you have to train for the Olympics. It simply means that you go for a walk for a half hour each day or engage in something more vigorous.

The best time to exercise is first thing in the morning, right after you get up, for thirty to sixty minutes. When you exercise in the morning, you pump freshly oxygenated blood to your brain, which makes you more alert and creative all day long.

Another important factor in sales success is your level of energy. In public speaking, your level of energy is perhaps the most important ingredient for success—and in selling it is the same.

Get Lots of Rest

The rule is this: If you are going to work five days per week, go to bed *early* five days per week. You need seven to eight hours of sleep each night, and perhaps more, if you are going to be fully rested and capable of making high-quality sales calls all day long.

ACTION EXERCISES

1. Resolve today to make every minute count. Calculate your hourly rate and then discipline yourself to do only those things that pay you the kind of money that you want to earn.

2. Select one habit from those suggested in this chapter that can help you the most to be more effective in your sales profession. Begin to develop that habit today and keep practicing it for twenty-one days until it is locked in and becomes automatic and easy.

FIVE

Develop Excellent Product Knowledge

YOUR LEVEL OF product knowledge is the foundation of credibility, confidence, and sales competence. Without extensive and detailed knowledge about what you are selling, no sales success is possible. The very best salespeople know their products and services inside and out, and can describe them in detail even without their sales materials or brochures.

Make sure that nobody can ask you a question about your product or service that you can't answer clearly and persuasively.

When you are clearly an expert on your product and how your product can help your customers improve their life or work, when you can clearly and thoroughly answer any question or concern that the prospect might have about what you are offering, and when it is clear that you have a deep conviction about the goodness and value of what you sell, your credibility goes up.

Know Your Customer

Once you know your product inside and out, the next step in product knowledge is for you to know your customer. Rather than trying to call on or sell to everyone, you should instead think through carefully the very best potential customer for what you sell.

There are three types of information that you must be clear about before you begin selling:

1. *Demographics.* Describe your ideal or perfect prospect. What is his age, education, occupation, stage of family formation, and previous experience with your product or service. These are the foundation questions of the more than $8 billion that are spent on market research each year in America. For you to move to the top of your field in sales and income, you must be clear about the descriptive or demographic qualities of your customers before you set out. This makes it much easier for you to separate qualified prospects from unqualified prospects early in the conversation.

2. *Psychographics.* This area is perhaps the most important breakthrough area in selling today. It refers to what is going on inside the mind of your prospective customer. What are the customer's fears, hopes, desires, and ambitions? What problem does your product solve? What need does your product satisfy? What goal does your product help your prospect to achieve? Perhaps the best question of all is, "What problem or pain do your prospects have that they will pay you to take away?"

3. *Ethnographics.* This is a newer area of sales success, and it is emerging as one of the most powerful. It refers to exactly how and when your customers use your product or service. What role does your product or service have in your customer's life or work? By showing prospects that your product or service fits comfortably into their normal lifestyle, you make it far more attractive and easier to purchase.

Identify Your Competitor

Another part of product knowledge is for you to ask and answer this question: "Who is your competitor?"

Who sells a product or service that competes with yours? Who are your primary competitors and who are your secondary competitors?

Remember, each customer has only a certain amount of money. Every sales offer is an attempt to capture that amount of money from the customer. Therefore, every alternate expenditure of this limited amount of money on the part of your customer is a form of competition. In the final result, the customer decides to spend his limited funds on exactly that product or service that is more important and desirable to him than any other similar or competitive product or service at that moment. How can you offer and position your product or service as the very best choice at this moment, all things considered?

Your Customer's Perspective

In thinking about your competitors, the next question is, "Why does your customer or prospect buy from your competitor?" What are the advantages that your prospective customer perceives in shopping with your competitor? How could you offset those perceived advantages or benefits? How could you position your product or service as being the superior choice to the product/service offered by your competitors?

Many salespeople have become extraordinarily successful by asking and answering this question over and over, and then by using this information to identify new customers and to neutralize the buying desires of customers who are currently purchasing from their competitors.

ACTION EXERCISES

1. What are the three most important benefits, results, or outcomes that a customer will enjoy from purchasing and using your product or service?

2. What are the three most important qualities or characteristics of the ideal customer for what you are selling?

SIX

Analyze Your Competition

THE CHINESE MILITARY strategist Sun Tzu, in his book *The Art of War*, said: "The General who knows himself but not his enemy will win on occasion. The General who knows his enemy but not himself will win a few victories. The General who does not know himself and does not know his enemy will lose every battle, while the General who knows himself and knows his enemy will prevail in a hundred battles."

Your competitors have a simple strategy. They wake up each morning thinking about how they can put you and every other company that offers competing products and services out of business. They think continually about how they can take your customers away and keep them permanently. They think, talk, plan, and strategize regularly to offer better, faster, cheaper, easier, and more convenient products and services than you. They are willing to match your every offering, slash their prices, and even lose money if necessary to get your customer for the first time. To succeed against such competitors, you must think the same way and take the same actions.

Conduct a SWOT analysis on your competitors. SWOT stands for strengths, weaknesses, opportunities, and threats. Just as a lawyer prepares the case from his opposition's point of view before he prepares his own case, you should prepare your marketing strategy by carefully studying your competitors.

Just as a commanding general of an army takes an enormous amount of time to study the disposition of the enemy before developing his own strategy, you should do the same thing.

In what ways is your competition superior to you? What are they doing to attract your potential customers away? Why is it that your prospective customers choose to buy from your competitor rather than from you? And how could you offset these advantages?

Determine Their Strengths and Weaknesses

What are the strengths of your competitors? Why is your competitor doing well in this difficult market? What is he offering, and how is he offering it? What is he doing well?

Here is an important life lesson: Always admire your successful competitors. When you admire your successful competitors, and respect them for the intelligent things that they do to attract and keep customers, you are much more likely to learn and improve your own business processes, so you can conduct your business at an even higher level than before.

Many people in business, and many salespeople, make a habit of criticizing or disparaging their successful competitors. As a result, they never learn from the smart things that their competitors are doing to become so successful. But when you admire your successful competitors and look for ways to learn from them, you advance much more rapidly in your field.

Next, consider their weaknesses. Where is your competitor inferior to you? Why is it that your customers buy from you rather than from your competitors?

Do Your Own Research

Here is a simple double-barreled marketing research technique that you can use tomorrow morning. First, call back your last ten customers, the ones who bought from you, and say these words: "I just wanted to call you and thank you for your decision to buy from us. We appreciate it very much. We are doing some market research here at the company and I was just wondering if you could answer a question for me? The question is this: What was the *one reason* that you decided to buy from us rather than buying from one of our competitors?"

You will be amazed to find that eight out of ten customers bought from you for the same reason. You'll often be more amazed to find that you did not know this reason when you made the sale. Most salespeople in most companies are not truly aware of why their customers decided to buy from them in the first place rather than from someone else.

With the information gleaned from this simple ten-customer survey, you will be able to focus on the primary reason people are buying. You can then incorporate this information into your sales work and all of your advertising and promotion.

Call Your Noncustomers

Second, call your last ten noncustomers, those prospective customers who decided to buy from your competitor rather than from you. Say these words: "Hello, this is John Salesman. I just wanted to call you and thank you for considering buying our product or service. I very much respect your decision to buy from someone else. I was hoping that you could give me some insights into the advantages and disadvantages you perceived with our product. Tell me, what was the one reason that you decided to buy from our competitor rather than from us?"

Then, remain perfectly silent. Almost invariably the customers will give you the one single reason why they decided to buy elsewhere. Whatever their reply, thank them again for their time, and tell them you hope that you will have a chance to do business with them again in the future.

You will often be astonished at the answer. If you had known beforehand what the primary buying motivation of the customer was, you could probably have offset it with a different offer or benefit. But because you did not know, the customer went somewhere else.

What About *You*?

Now analyze your own strengths and weaknesses. What are the strongest elements of your product or service as they relate to your customers' deepest wants and needs? Where do you get the most compliments from your customers on your products or services? What makes your customers the happiest when they buy and use your products or services? You must be crystal clear about the answers to these questions.

Where is your product or service weak in comparison with your competitors? What is it that you need to change or improve in order to offset this weakness? What can you do immediately to compensate for this weakness so that it is no longer an obstacle to a customer buying from you rather than from someone else?

All good marketing strategy is aimed at identifying where your competitor is superior and taking steps to compensate for that strength, and meanwhile identifying where your competitor is weak, and exploiting that weakness.

ACTION EXERCISES

1. Who is your most successful competitor? List three advantages or benefits that your competitor offers to your customers that you do not currently offer.

2. What are the three greatest strengths of your product or service, and how could you convey these benefits with greater clarity to your prospective customers?

SEVEN

Develop Competitive Advantage

THE MOST important factor in successful selling is the development of a *competitive advantage*. For you to sell successfully, customers must be convinced that what you offer is superior and more desirable than the offerings of your competitors. Differentiation is the key to sales success.

What is your competitive advantage today? What makes your product superior to any other similar product in the minds of your customer?

Your Area of Excellence

What is your area of excellence? What does your product or service offer to a customer that makes it the most desirable choice, all things considered? What is the main benefit of buying and using your product or service that makes it a better choice than that of any of your competitors?

The competitive advantage offered by your product or service, or your company, is the heart of all your marketing and sales efforts. It is the reason that you survive and thrive in a competitive marketplace. It is the key to your success. As Peter Drucker said, "If you don't have a competitive advantage, you must immediately go to work to develop one."

If you're not sure, or if your product does not have a competitive advantage, ask yourself: What could it be? What should it be, if you want to be successful in the long term?

Unique Added Value

Michael Porter, the Harvard expert on competitive advantage, says that you must have a "unique added value" for your customers.

It is not necessary that you be superior to all of your competitors. It is only necessary that you offer something special, different, and more valuable to the specific customers that you have decided to serve.

With what customers does your competitive advantage make a real difference? Almost every product or service has certain advantages that make it a better choice for certain customers. Let us say that you sell Cadillacs. Cadillacs have a competitive advantage because they are luxury cars with a reputation and image for quality. But you have to ask yourself, "With what customers is this competitive advantage important?"

The desirable qualities of a Cadillac would most appeal to people who can afford to buy and drive luxury cars. Your market is not people who drive Fords, Chevrolets, or Subarus. Your market is the high-end customer with discretionary income.

Therefore, what unique added value does a Cadillac have that makes it a superior choice over BMW, and Audi, or Mercedes-Benz?

To safely lead your field in a competitive market, your product must be different and superior in at least four ways:

1. *Your product could offer better quality.* But quality is defined by your customer. How does your customer define quality?

2. *Your product could work faster and get better results.* By what method does your product or service get faster results than your competitor's offering? Why is that meaningful, in financial or personal terms, to your customer? What difference does it make in the life or work of your customer that your product or service delivers results or benefits faster than your competitors?

3. *Your product could be cheaper.* It could be cheaper than your competitor's product in terms of the cost of purchase. It could be cheaper in terms of the lifelong cost of owning the product. If it is cheaper, what does this mean to your customer and why is it to the customer's advantage to buy

from you at a lower price than to buy from your competitor at a higher price?

4. *Your product could be easier or more convenient.* Customers are lazy in that they always prefer a product or a service that is easier to use than one that is more difficult. In what way is your product or service easier to use? Why is it easier? How is it easier? What difference does it make in the life or work of your customer? If all of sales success revolves around your ability to differentiate your product or service from those of your competitors, and to ensure that it appears to be a more desirable choice, who are your competitors?

Maximize Your Strengths

All sales success revolves around your ability to differentiate your product or service from those of your competitors, and ensure that it appears to be a more desirable choice. Who, then, are your competitors? Why do your customers buy from your competitors? What advantages do they see? In what ways do they feel that your competitor's product or service is superior to yours?

Especially, in all honesty, in what ways are your competitor's products/services better than yours? How can you offset the advantages that your competitors have, or the advantages that your customers perceive that they have? What could you say or do to present your product or service in such a way that you maximize your strengths and emphasize your competitor's weaknesses and vulnerabilities?

In many cases, products and services are similar. Think of restaurants offering the same kind of food. In this case, the way that you differentiate yourself is by offering better, warmer, friendlier customer service. In many cases, especially where a product or service is perceived as a commodity that's available everywhere, the quality of customer service is the competitive advantage that gives you an edge in the customer's mind.

Sometimes, all you need to win the customer is to be superior in one specific area that the customer considers important.

Here is an exercise for you: On the back of your business card, write a ten- to fifteen-word reason that would cause a skeptical, well-informed customer to buy from you rather than from someone else.

If you cannot write your competitive advantage on the back of a business card, it is quite possible that you do not know what it is, or you are not capable of articulating your competitive advantage in a sales situation.

ACTION EXERCISES

1. List two reasons why your product or service is superior to that of any of your competitors.

2. List two results, benefits, or improvements that your customer will enjoy when they buy your product, as opposed to buying a similar product from a competitor.

EIGHT

Develop an Effective Sales Strategy

ONE OF THE characteristics of top salespeople is that they engage in long-term thinking. Instead of reacting and responding to what is going on around them each day, they take some time to stand back and look at their market from the point of view of a general surveying the battlefield.

Top salespeople, first of all, become thoroughly familiar with their product or service, and what it can do better than any other competitive product or service to change or improve the life or work of the customer.

Then, the top salespeople survey the marketplace to develop as much clarity as possible about exactly those customers who would be most likely to buy, use, and enjoy what they are selling.

Four Pillars of Selling Strategy

There are four key concepts of a successful selling strategy:

1. *Specialization.* You may have many products or services, and different sizes, shapes, and ingredients in the items that you sell. To be successful, it is essential that you specialize and sell just one or a few products or services in a superior fashion. You cannot sell everything, so you need to become excellent in selling just a few things. Which products or services should you focus on?

It is true that the world around you is full of prospects, but not all of them are *your* prospects. Your second area of specialization therefore has to do with the type of customers that you are going to sell to. You will always be most comfortable selling to people who are very much like you. They will be similar to you in education, background, experience, worldview, even lifestyle and dress. Your ideal customer is someone who you will naturally be comfortable with, and who will be comfortable with you.

You can also specialize in a particular geographical area. One of the best salesmen I ever met changed from selling for IBM to selling and leasing commercial property. His office was in a downtown building. He got a map of the downtown area in which commercial properties were concentrated, and then drew a circle around his office that embraced five minutes of walking in any direction. He resolved that he would work only in this area, which consisted of hundreds of office buildings and prospective tenants, and only work with clients whose offices were within a five-minute walk from his office. With this philosophy, and an intense focus on this tight geographical area, he earned more than $200,000 in his first year while other salesmen around him were struggling.

Therefore, you can specialize in a particular type of product or service that your company offers, a particular type of customer, or a particular region or area of activity. This is the first step in setting sales strategy.

2. *Differentiation.* Once you have decided on the product or service in which you will specialize, you then look around you to determine exactly those prospects who would be most likely to buy from you, based on your area of differentiation and superiority.

Each customer makes a buying decision, a choice between competitive products, usually based on *one* main advantage or benefit that he is convinced he will receive. Your job is to determine what unique added value or special benefit your product or service can offer, and what particular type of customers value that benefit so much that they would choose you over all other competitors and all other products available.

You can differentiate yourself in terms of product knowledge as well. One of the reasons that people buy a product or service is because they are convinced that the salesperson is an expert in that product or service area. They have more confidence buying from a person who seems to know more about his product or service than a competitor might.

You can also differentiate yourself on the basis of the superiority of your sales skills. The biggest and best companies learned long ago that the quality of the training they give their salespeople will largely determine the success of those salespeople against the competition.

3. *Segmentation.* What market segments or groups of customers can benefit the most from your areas of specialization and differentiation? Write out a description of your ideal or perfect customer. What are the *demographics*? What is the customer's age, education, position, level of family formation, and current lifestyle?

Analyze the *psychographics* of your ideal customer. What are the customer's hopes, fears, desires, problems, goals, and aspirations for the future? You then look for more and more people who fit the ideal customer profile. The greater clarity you have with regard to what constitutes an ideal customer, the more of them you will find, and the easier you will be able to sell to them.

4. *Concentration.* This pillar of success requires that you focus single-mindedly on selling your products and services to just those customers or customer groups who can and will buy and pay the soonest, and who will most appreciate the special features and benefits that your product offers. Where should you concentrate your sales energies so that you can make more sales, faster and easier than you might be today?

Focus and Concentration Pay Off

Here is an example from my own experience. A friend of mine graduated from college and decided to get into the insurance industry. Once he had completed his training and had received his license, he began cold-calling on a wide variety of possible prospects.

Of course, the best prospects are those people who are earning a high income, consistently, and do not have the time or knowledge to make good choices and decisions about life insurance and financial planning. He soon found that all of the other agents were thinking the same way. As a result, they focused most of their efforts on lawyers, architects, engineers, doctors, dentists, medical specialists, and business owners. As they say, "Fish where the fish are."

He decided that, in order to stand out from this crowd of competitive salespeople, he had to specialize in a particular type of customer, and in a particular type of insurance and financial planning. He settled upon life insurance and estate planning, and decided to focus on doctors and dentists and other medical professionals.

He then devoted himself to becoming an expert in the medical profession in order to differentiate himself from his fellow salespeople. He interviewed doctors, attended medical association meetings, read medical magazines and papers, and eventually developed a complete understanding of the financial needs, requirements, and problems of doctors.

Develop a Reputation

Over the course of about two years, he developed a reputation for being perhaps the most knowledgeable financial planner and insurance specialist for medical professionals. He was invited to speak and give seminars at medical conferences on the specific problems facing medical professionals, and the very best ways to organize their financial lives.

Within five years, he was one of the top insurance agents in the world, earning more than a million dollars a year in straight commission work by specializing, differentiating, segmenting, and then concentrating on exactly those customers who represented the highest potential income for him in his business.

ACTION EXERCISES

1. In what product or service area do you specialize, and what are the most important benefits that a person enjoys from purchasing that product or service from you?

2. What are the characteristics and qualities of your ideal customer—the one who most appreciates and values the products and services in which you specialize?

NINE

Prospect Like a Professional

FINDING NEW people to buy your product or service is the most important part of the sales process. Your ability to prospect effectively—to find people who want and need your product or service, and are willing to buy and pay for it in the short term—is the key to your success.

Buying Results, Not Products

People do not buy products or services. They buy results or benefits. They buy the change or improvement that they expect to enjoy as the result of purchasing your product or service. Start the prospecting process by sitting down and making a list of all the benefits that a customer could enjoy by using your product or service in different ways.

If you have a variety of benefits, organize them by priority and determine the greatest single benefit that a customer would experience. In addition, if your product offers several benefits, each of these benefits may appeal to a different type of customer.

The next stage in prospecting is for you to define exactly the prospect or person who would be most likely to buy your product or service, and buy it *immediately*. This requires that you define your product or service in one of four different ways.

What's the Problem You Can Solve?

First, what problem would an ideal customer have that your product can solve? You are looking for people who have a problem that they are willing to pay you to solve for them. You uncover this problem by asking good questions and listening closely to the answers.

Problems fall into three categories. The first is that they are obvious and clear. The customer knows she has a problem and knows what it is.

The second is that they are not obvious and are unclear. The prospect has a problem but does not know what it is and therefore is unclear about what to do to solve it. One of the great breakthrough areas in modern selling is when you can show customers that they have a problem that they did not know they had, and how you can take that problem away in a cost-effective manner.

The third type of problem is the *nonexistent* problem. Quite often, when you call on a prospect, seeking a person who has a problem that your product can solve, you find that the customer really does not have that problem at all. They do not need what you are selling. They are doing just fine as they are.

Find the Key Need

Second, you look for prospects who have a need that has not yet been fulfilled. Needs are what trigger buying desire and buying behavior. Many people have needs but do not know that there is a product you can sell them that would satisfy that need. This is usually why they greet an initial sales approach with words such as, "I'm not interested," or "I'm not in the market right now."

Exactly what need does your product or service satisfy that your customer is willing to pay you for?

Identify Their Goals

The third quality of good prospects is that they have a goal that they have not yet been able to achieve. It can be anything from weight loss to financial independence, to higher income and more rapid promotion in their job. *What goal* can your product or service uniquely help the customer achieve?

One of the best questioning strategies is to ask customers about their long-term goals. The greater clarity that people have about the goals that they wish to achieve, the better prospects they will be and the faster they will buy what you are selling—as long as your product helps them to achieve those goals in a cost-effective way.

Where Does It Hurt?

Finally, you are looking for a prospect who has a pain, concern, worry, or stress that you can help to alleviate or take away. A simple question such as "What keeps you awake at night?" will often open up a torrent of selling opportunities.

In the final analysis, from the time of the ancient Sumerian markets of 5,000 B.C., customers have only and always bought one thing: *improvement.*

What improvement in the life or work of your customer does your product or service offer? Customers buy in anticipation of how much better off they will be after they have bought and used your product than they were before they experienced it. You must be clear about the benefit or improvement, and you must make it clear to your customers that they will enjoy that benefit or improvement.

Business to Business Selling

If you sell to businesses, their needs are very simple. They want to either *increase* their sales and profitability, or to *decrease* their costs and expenses. They want to save or gain time or money. They want to improve their business operations in some way.

Business customers determine the value of your product or service, and what they are willing to pay, by the *difference* between the price you charge and the financial benefits they will enjoy as the result. Both must be clear to your prospects before they can make a buying decision.

The good news is that if you ask enough questions and listen carefully to the answers, your prospects will tell you everything you need to know to present your product as the best choice for them, all things considered.

The Hundred Call Method

One of the biggest challenges of prospecting is overcoming the fear of rejection. To overcome this fear of rejection, there is a simple technique that you can use. Resolve today to use what I call the "hundred call method."

This method requires that you go out immediately and call on 100 new prospects as fast as you possibly can. The difference here is that you do not really care very much whether or not they buy. Your focus is on the number of prospects that you call on, not your sales results.

There seems to be a wonderful point of balance between wanting the sale too much and wanting the sale too little. When you achieve that point of balance, where you want the sale but you don't particularly care if it comes through, you become the most effective salesperson you can possibly be.

When you implement the hundred call method in your life, and you call on 100 different people as quickly as you can, at the end of the process you will have become totally *fearless*. With regard to rejection, you will have ice water in your veins. You will be totally unafraid of calling on anybody at any time. For the rest of your career you will actually look forward to prospecting because you know that every prospecting call moves you one step closer to a successful sale.

ACTION EXERCISES

1. Identify your ideal customers, and the problem, need, or goal they have that will cause them to buy from you.

2. Resolve today to double your "face time" and spend more time each day with prospects who can and will buy from you in a short period of time.

TEN

Qualify Your Prospects

ONE OF THE GREATEST time wasters in the business of selling is spending too much time with people who cannot or will not buy your product or service. Your ability to qualify your prospects clearly at the beginning of the conversation, even over the telephone, can save you an enormous amount of time, and increase your income substantially.

Customers today are overwhelmed with as many as 5,000 commercial messages per day, all saying, "Buy me! Buy me! Buy me!"

Getting Customer Attention

The scarcest single resource in business is customer attention. For you to get a chance to sell or to *score*, you must break through your prospective customers' preoccupations so that they are willing to listen to you in the first place.

Whenever possible, open your sales conversation with a strong question that qualifies the prospect immediately and gets the person's attention. Ask a question to which a *Yes* answer qualifies the person as a possible prospect who might buy and use your product or service.

For example, when selling to businesses, you could open with, "Would you like see an idea that could make (or save) you a lot of time or money?"

Since the primary concern of people in business is to save or gain time or money, this type of a question should immediately get their attention. Most products or services that you sell to a business will somehow offer a financial benefit—a way to increase sales and profitability or to decrease costs and expenses.

If you are selling residential real estate, a good opening question would be, "Are you looking for an ideal home in a quiet neighborhood?"

Since this simple question embraces the desires and concerns of 90 percent of residential real estate buyers, the prospect will almost invariably say, "Of course, that's exactly what we're looking for."

If you are approaching a sales manager whose income is determined by the success of the sales force, your approach could be something that I used for years: "Would you be interested in a way to increase your sales by 20 percent to 30 percent over the next six to twelve months?"

This question almost always elicited the ideal response: "Of course. What is it?"

If your opening question does not elicit the "What is it?" response, then you must go back to the drawing board and work on your opening question until it elicits that response every time from a qualified prospect.

Focus on the Prospect

In your initial contact with the prospect, focus all your attention and your questions on the prospect. Don't talk about who you are and what you do, or about your company. Remember, it is about them, not about you.

Client-centered selling is professional selling. You are only selling professionally when you are talking to your client about his or her wants and needs.

Question Your Way to Success

In prospecting, the more information that you can elicit, the easier it will be for you to qualify the prospect and then go on to make a sale. This is where questioning is so important. Your questions should be thought out carefully in advance, and organized in a logical sequence, from the most general to the most specific.

Once you have a positive response from a prospect to your opening question, you then ask him questions about his business, his market, his budget, and so on. Very often, people will give you all of this information in exchange for the benefit that you promised in your opening question.

Cold-Calling Strategy

When you are cold-calling, or calling on a prospect for the first time, a strategy is for you to "go in naked."

What this means is that, at the most, you carry a simple folder rather than a briefcase full of brochures or samples. If the prospect is interested and wants a presentation and more information, you can always go back to your car to get what you need and bring it in. But when you go in without a briefcase you lower the stress of initial sales resistance and cause the prospect to relax and open up to you sooner.

In your first call, you should never attempt to sell. Focus on information gathering. Unless you are selling something inexpensive that requires little thought, you want to interview the prospect and ask questions. Take notes and tell them you will come back to them if you think that you have some ideas that can help them. Focus on building the relationship and coming across as friendly, genial, and nonthreatening.

The longer that your prospect remains relaxed, and the more he opens up to you, the more likely it is you will make the sale in the long run.

Identify the Key Benefit

With each customer, there is a key benefit that will trigger buying desire and cause the customer to purchase your product or service. At the same time, there is a key fear or doubt that will hold the customer back from buying. Your initial job in the prospecting conversation, and the key to qualifying, is to find out exactly what benefit will cause this customer to buy from you, and exactly what fear or doubt might hold this customer back from buying from you.

Don't be afraid to ask. "Ask" is the magic word for sales success. You can even say, "Mr. Prospect, what we have found is that there is always a key benefit or major reason that a person would purchase our product or service. What might it be for you?"

If you are open, honest, and genuine, and ask out of curiosity, you will be amazed at the answers you'll hear. Prospects will often give you all the information that you need to make a sale. The key is for you to ask.

ACTION EXERCISES

1. Develop an opening question or statement that allows you to determine if this is a good prospect for what you sell.

2. Identify the key benefit that your ideal customer seeks, and be sure to offer it in your opening words.

ELEVEN

The Friendship Factor

IN THOUSANDS of interviews, when customers are asked to think of the words that best describe how they feel about the top salespeople who call on them, the first and most important word is always "friend."

"I see her as a friend," the customer will say, or "I feel that he is more interested in me and in helping me achieve my goals than he is in just making a sale."

Earlier, we called this "relationship selling," referring to the importance of establishing a high-quality, credible, trust-based relationship with the prospect before you make any attempt to persuade him to buy or use your product or service. In this case, as Shakespeare said, "Make haste slowly."

Focus on the Friendship

Friendship is an essential requirement, and the foundation of professional selling. It is based on the very simple conclusion that people will not buy from you until they are convinced that you are their friend and that you are acting in their best interests.

The first job you have to do in the selling process is to establish *trust.* You do this by being on time, being prepared, and by focusing single-mindedly on the customer at the beginning of the sales process. From a foundation of trust, you move gradually to a feeling of friendship. The basic rule is that you cannot sell to someone you do not like, and you cannot buy from someone you don't like, either. If we don't like and trust the person we are talking to, no matter how attractive the product or service, we will seldom buy it. Liking, trusting, and friendship are the foundations of relationship selling.

The Doctor of Selling

One way to build trust, confidence, and friendship with the prospect is to take what I call the doctor of selling approach. This requires that you think about yourself as if you were a "doctor of sales," a complete professional with a high code of ethics.

If you visit a doctor for any reason, anywhere in the world, every legitimate doctor will always follow a three part process: *examination*, *diagnosis*, and *prescription.*

In videotaped interviews of sales conversations, it seems that the top salespeople in every field follow the same process in the sales conversation.

THE EXAMINATION
In the examination, the doctor will spend a good deal of time asking you questions, taking blood tests and blood pressure

and other diagnostic parameters to fully understand your condition. During the examination phase, the doctor does not suggest different courses of treatment or prescriptions that you can take. The doctor focuses single-mindedly on one thing: asking questions, doing tests, and fully understanding your true needs or situation.

In professional selling, the examination phase is when you ask well-prepared questions that move from the general to the particular about the customer's needs, wants, concerns, problems, and goals. The more time that you take to conduct a thorough examination, or what we call the "need identification phase," the more the customer will like and trust you and feel that you are acting in his best interests. The more he will like you.

THE DIAGNOSIS

The second part of the doctor of selling approach is the diagnosis. This is when you summarize your findings, as a doctor would when he gets tests back from the lab, and explain to the patient (customer) exactly what you feel is that person's true problem or need. Good doctors always take the time to carefully explain their findings and the potential interpretations of these findings.

Once the customer (patient) fully understands that he has a problem or need that should be dealt with, the next part of the conversation is the presentation of your product or service.

THE PRESCRIPTION

In the third phase of the doctor of selling approach, which we call the prescription, you present your product or service persuasively as being exactly the right solution to the problem or need that you and the customer have mutually identified.

In the prescription phase, you present your product or service, answer questions or concerns that the customer might have, show that your recommended course of treatment is the best and most effective approach to solving the person's problem, all things considered, and then go on to arrange the necessary treatment—or in selling, to get the customer to take action.

The Relationship Is Everything

If the relationship is strong enough between you and your doctor, you will often accept the doctor's recommendations the first time he gives them, and actually be eager to begin the treatment so that you can solve the problem or take away the needs.

To develop a friendly and trust-based relationship with your patient, you should take a low-key, professional, client-centered, and client-focused approach. Concentrate on building trust and friendship by focusing single-mindedly on the customer and how you can help him or her solve a problem or achieve a goal. The more time you take to thoroughly understand the real needs of your customer, the easier it is to present your product or service as the ideal solution.

Caring, Courtesy, and Respect

A truly friendly relationship is based on caring, courtesy, and respect. You express how much you care by asking questions about the customer's life or work, and then by listening carefully and sympathetically to the answers. You express courtesy by always being polite, not only with the customer, but with everyone in the customer's office or home with whom you deal.

Finally, you express respect by asking intelligent questions, listening attentively to the answers, making recommendations, and always asking the customer for feedback on what you are selling. The more you focus on "selling without selling," the faster you will build the friendship factor into your sales relationship, and the more likely you will be to make the sale and keep the sale at the end of the conversation.

ACTION EXERCISES

1. To build a friendlier relationship faster, imagine that your customer is a fascinating person with a rich inner life. Ask questions and listen expectantly, as though this person is about to say something profound and moving.

2. In your next sales meeting, put aside any desire to make a sale and instead concentrate on really understanding your customer, relative to your product or service, in as much detail as possible.

TWELVE

Three Keys to Persuasion

PSYCHOLOGISTS have identified a variety of things that you can do to speed up the decision-making process that leads to a sale. In the normal buying process, the prospect sees and talks to the salesperson, often several times, and then carefully considers the pros and cons of buying or not buying. After what is often an extended process, the customer will finally come full circle to the point of agreeing to purchase your product or service.

Use Proven Sales Triggers

However, researchers have found that there are certain psychological "triggers" that you can *pull* in the sales conversation that will cause the customer to buy from you almost immediately. These triggers are used in most successful marketing and advertising activities to move people from being completely uninterested to having a desire to buy, sometimes within the time span of a thirty- or sixty-second television commercial. You can do the same in your selling work.

Many years of research in motivational psychology have been devoted to uncovering some of the reasons people behave the way they do, especially in sales situations. The research shows that each customer has deep subconscious needs that must be satisfied before a purchase decision is made. Buying influences are like triggers that bring about rapid buying decisions. They connect immediately with these subconscious needs. The use of these triggers short-cuts the decision-making process.

The Power of Reciprocity

The first and most powerful buying influence is *reciprocity*. We have a deep need to "square things" with other people, to give back for whatever they do for us or to us. We like to repay others when they do something nice for us. We want to reciprocate for the kindnesses or favors of others.

The first type of reciprocity is *emotional* reciprocity: "If you make me feel good, I'll make you feel good." You can trigger this feeling by being a nice person, asking good questions, listening attentively, and making the prospect feel important.

In *physical* reciprocity, we say, "If you do something nice for me, or give me something nice of a physical nature, I'll do something nice for you or repay you in some way."

Always look for ways to do favors or kindnesses for your prospects. Send thank-you cards on every occasion to build goodwill with your prospects. When you show kindness, caring, and courtesy to people, and listen to them carefully when they talk so that they feel better and happier about themselves, they want to reciprocate in some way—and often it's by carefully considering and even buying what you are selling.

Commitment and Consistency

The second key buying influence or emotional buying trigger is called *commitment and consistency*.

The Law of Incremental Commitment applies to all customers in sales activities. This means that they begin with zero commitment when they first meet you and talk to you. It then takes them a certain amount of time to move to 100 percent commitment, where they buy your product or service. You must give people sufficient time to move across the spectrum from zero interest to convinced customer.

People also strive to remain consistent with what they have done and said in the past. When you ask customers thoughtful questions about their situation and then show them that your product or service exactly answers those questions and solves the problems the customer has identified, the sale becomes much easier. People don't argue with their own data.

People strive to remain consistent with the image that they have of themselves. When you say, "All the top companies are switching to this product or service," you trigger within your customers' mind the desire to purchase your product or service because they see themselves and think of themselves as one of the "top companies."

When you say that "all really successful people are using this product or service now," individuals whose self-image is tied to being successful are immediately more interested in purchasing what you are selling than they were before.

What Others Say and Do

A third major buying trigger is called *social proof.* It is one of the most powerful of all buying influences. Human beings are social animals. They are greatly influenced by what other people around them are doing and saying. Prospects are inordinately influenced by other people similar to them who have bought your product or service.

One of the first questions that a customer asks, whether expressed aloud or not, is, "Who else that I know and respect has bought this product?"

Social proof is so powerful that it can cause a prospect to turn around 180 degrees, from having zero interest to wanting to purchase immediately.

The customer feels that if other people similar to him have bought the product, it must be a good choice. The customer assumes that the other intelligent customer has already done his homework for him. The other customer has already thought through the product or service, carefully evaluated it, and reached an intelligent buying decision. He is therefore safe to do the same.

Another part of social proof is testimonial letters, lists, photos, and increasingly, videos from happy customers talking about how good your product or service is, and how happy they are to have purchased it and to be using it. The more people who can testify to the goodness of what you sell, the safer and easier it is for an interested prospect to buy the product from you.

ACTION EXERCISES

1. Identify one or two things that you can do or say, or even present as a gift to your prospect on the first call, to trigger the person's desire to reciprocate by listening to you and perhaps even buying what you sell.

2. Develop two concrete examples of other people who have purchased your product and have been very happy with the results and the benefits that they enjoyed. Talk about these customers during your sales presentation.

THIRTEEN

Make Effective Presentations

THE PRESENTATION is the "inner game" of selling, where the actual sale is made. It is during the presentation when you transform a skeptical or reluctant prospect into a committed customer.

An effective presentation can increase your sales by several times over an unplanned and uncoordinated explanation of your product or service.

Once you have determined that the prospect needs the product, can use the product, can benefit from the product, and can afford the product, it is time to persuade the prospect to take action.

Fully 95 percent of presentations can be improved upon in some way. Keep working on your presentation until you sell successfully to a qualified prospect almost every time.

Follow a Logical Process

The presentation is a logical, orderly way of moving from the general to the specific. Before you begin, you will have gone through the process of clearly determining that this person is a prospect for what you are selling, building a positive relationship based on friendship and trust, and analyzing the customer's needs carefully so that the customer is clear about how she can benefit from what you are selling.

Remember, selling out of sequence can kill the sale. Starting to talk about your product before the customer is clear that she has a need or a problem that your product can satisfy or solve will cause the prospect to lose interest and say, "I'm not really interested at this time," or "Leave it with me. Let me look at it," or even worse, "Let me think it over."

Before you begin your presentation, make sure that the environment is ideal for you to present and for the customer to pay attention and listen. People can only focus on one thing at a time. If there are distractions, interruptions, or noise of any kind, the prospect will be unable to concentrate on what you are saying, and therefore unable to buy at the end of your presentation.

The Presentation Formula

Plan your presentation thoroughly in advance. Think on paper. Review your presentation prior to every customer meeting, no matter how often you have given it in the past. Remember, preparation is the mark of the professional.

The best formula for making a sales presentation is to "show, tell, and ask questions."

Show the prospect what your product is and, especially, what it does to change or improve the life or work of the prospect in some way. *Tell* the prospect how he or she will benefit. Then, *ask a question* to be sure that what you are presenting is important or relevant: "Is this something you would use? Would this be an improvement on what you are currently doing?"

Teach the prospect how he or she can most benefit from enjoying and using your product or service. Create exciting mental pictures of the prospect smiling and benefiting from your product: "Just imagine yourself using this product or service every day. What kind of a difference would that make in your life or work?"

The Principle of Three

Another powerful presentation technique is what we call the principle of three.

Because of this (describe the product feature), *you can* (describe the product benefit), *which means* (describe the customer benefit).

For example, if you were selling a flat-screen TV, you would say, "Because of this new flat-screen technology [product feature], you can mount this TV on any wall [product benefit], which means that you can turn your living room into a theater for your family and friends [customer benefit]."

Tell Stories

Perhaps the most powerful tool that you can use in making a persuasive presentation is what is called "anecdotal selling."

This is when you reinforce your presentation with stories and examples of other customers who have bought from you, and who are happy with your product or service.

Tell lots of success stories about your happy customers. The reason why this technique is so powerful is because all buying decisions are made in the right brain, and the right brain is activated by pictures, images, and stories of different kinds.

When you tell a success story about a happy customer, your potential customers automatically project themselves into the story of that customer and see themselves enjoying your product or service as well.

ACTION EXERCISES

1. Make a list of every "success story" enjoyed by people who have bought your product or service, whether it is your story or the story of someone else. Use these stories often.

2. Resolve to plan, prepare, and review your presentation carefully, right before every sales conversation.

FOURTEEN

Practice the Power of Suggestion

PEOPLE ARE greatly influenced by the power of the suggestive elements in their environment. Nowhere is this more important than in the selling process. By clearly identifying the suggestive elements that you can control, and then by employing them consistently in every sales conversation, you can have a more consistent and positive influence on the buying behavior of the prospect.

There are certain things that you can do as a salesperson that can have a strong subconscious and suggestive impact on the behavior of your prospect. Remember the rule, "Everything counts!" Everything that you do in the sales conversation either helps or hurts. Everything you do or say in the presence of the customer either moves you closer to a sale or moves you further away. Everything counts.

Personality Is Important

The first suggestive element is your personality and how you relate to the customer. When you are positive, warm, friendly, and demonstrate a cheerful attitude, you have a positive suggestive influence on the customer. The customer is more open to listen to you and to be persuaded by you.

The depth of your belief in the goodness of your product or service, and in your company, also has a powerful, positive suggestive influence. When you combine a belief in the goodness of your product with a clear desire to help to improve the life or work of your customer, the customer is greatly influenced and persuaded, especially at an unconscious level.

Your Voice Is Vital

Speaking clearly is a strong suggestive influence. People who speak up and raise their volume on the last words of each sentence have a far greater impact than people whose voices drop.

When you speak with clarity and confidence, it sounds like your product or service is of greater value and is superior to that represented by someone who speaks in a softer tone. Make sure that your diction and elocution are crisp and clear.

How You Appear

Your visual impact on the customer is extremely important. Fully 95 percent of the first impression you make will be determined by your clothes. Human beings are intensely visual. Experts say that they make their first conclusion about you within four seconds of seeing you for the first time.

Be sure that you are attractively groomed and well dressed when you meet with a prospect. You don't have to be handsome or beautiful. Average-looking salespeople are more successful than handsome or beautiful salespeople who may cause the prospect to be distracted in some way.

Dress for Success

But the rule is that you must "dress for success." You must look your best. You must be properly groomed and attractively attired. You must look like a successful person working for a successful company, selling a successful product. Even people who are not particularly well dressed or physically fit themselves like to deal with people who are.

When I was a young salesman, poorly dressed and ignorant of the impact of my appearance on my prospects, I was taken aside by a senior salesman. He asked me if I would like a little advice or input on my appearance. Fortunately, I had no ego problems. I told him I was open to any advice he could give me that would help me to be more successful.

He sat down with me and gave me a tutorial on proper business dress. To this day, I still remember him "schooling me." From then on, I acquired matching shirts and ties, wore polished shoes, and groomed more correctly for my audience. In a very short period of time, I noticed that people treated me with greater respect, listened to me with greater intensity, and bought my product in larger quantities. It was a real eye-opener for me.

The First Impression

People make their first impression of you in *four* seconds and then finalize their impressions of you within thirty seconds. After that, they engage in what psychologists call "confirmation bias." They look for reasons to justify their first impressions. If you don't make a good impression with your appearance in the first thirty seconds, you will be swimming upstream and find yourself struggling to get the attention and respect of the customer. This is especially true if you are dealing with successful people. They are more critical and judgmental than almost anyone else.

Put Your Product in Its Best Light

The fourth element in your suggestive toolbox is your *product*. Make sure that you display your product in its very best light. Be sure that all of your sales materials are clean, neat, and attractive. Your prospect assumes that the quality of your sales materials is a direct extension of the quality of the product that you're offering. Make sure that they look first-class.

In real estate there is a booming market for people who excel in what is called "home staging." A professional comes into a home that is for sale and recommends furniture removal or replacement, updates to carpets and countertops, and ideas to unclutter and make an entire home look beautiful and attractive to live in. This visual impression has an enormous impact on how appealing the home is, how much the purchaser will pay for the home, and how quickly the home sells.

Remember, in terms of the power of suggestion, everything that the customer sees, hears, or feels has an impact on the customer's final decision to buy your product or not. Everything counts.

ACTION EXERCISES

1. Resolve today that you are going to groom, dress, and present yourself as if you were the most successful and highest-paid person in your industry. How would you dress differently from the way you do right now?

2. Organize your sales presentation and sales materials so that they are clean, neat, attractive, and increase the buying desire of the customer.

FIFTEEN

Establish Megacredibility

THE AVERAGE customer is bombarded with hundreds and even thousands of commercial sales messages every day.

The customer is surrounded by people and companies trying to sell him or her products of all kinds, at all levels of quality and price. The customer today is therefore extremely skeptical and suspicious of any and all sales efforts.

For you to be successful in selling, you must develop a method of overcoming skepticism and building high levels of confidence in the mind of the customer toward you, your company, and your products and services. In short, you must learn how to develop high levels of credibility—what we call megacredibility—in everything you do that affects the customer and the buying decision.

Neutralize the Fear of Failure

The major obstacle to buying today is the fear of failure in the mind of the customer. Customers fear paying too much for your product or service. They are afraid of ending up with the wrong product for their particular needs, or making a buying mistake and being criticized by others for having bought something that is inappropriate or overpriced. Customers are afraid of getting stuck with a product that they cannot get serviced or repaired.

The reason that customers have these fears is because they have had this type of negative experience in the past, usually many times over the years. They are determined not to make the same mistakes again.

Trust Reduces Fear

The good news is that the more customers believe you and what you say, the lower their fear of making a mistake in a buying relationship. As the customer's trust in you grows on the one hand, the fear of making a mistake decreases on the other. Your central job therefore is to increase the customer's confidence and trust in you. This increases the likelihood that the customer will accept what you say and buy what you sell.

Everything you do in the sales relationship either helps or hurts in the building of trust and credibility. Everything either adds to or takes away from the credibility you need to make a sale. Customers are nervous and uneasy about making a wrong decision and will therefore interpret things in a negative way, if you allow them to.

Your main job is to position yourself as the low-risk provider of your product or service. Position yourself as the lowest risk rather than the lowest price seller. Customers will pay more to reduce risk in a purchase decision; if they have the choice of high risk accompanied by lower price or low risk accompanied by higher price, they will always move to higher price and lower risk.

Five Elements of Megacredibility

There are five key elements in the megacredibility that you require to make a sale:

1. *The Salesperson.* Your appearance, your behavior, your attitude, your clothes, and your grooming all raise or lower the customer's confidence in buying from you and your company.

2. *Your Reputation.* The most valuable asset that your company has is its reputation for quality products and services with other customers in the marketplace. It is said that fully 85 percent of the sales decision is based on what is called word-of-mouth. This means that someone else, either directly or indirectly, says that your product or service is good and that you, as the customer, should buy it.

Be sure to tell your prospect about the size of your company, how long you've been in business, and how large your market share has become because of your quality and service. Be sure that your brochures, handouts, sales materials, and business card all look first-class. Be sure that the telephone manners of you and your staff, and how quickly you respond to inquiries, are handled in an excellent way.

3. *Social Proof.* Perhaps nothing is more persuasive than stories of other customers in similar situations who have purchased your product and were happy with their decision.

The customer always wants to know, "Who else has purchased it?" and "What was their experience with your product or service?" Use testimonial letters, lists, photographs, and even videos of your happy customers. Best of all are stories of customers who might have hesitated to buy your product or service at first, but after they did, they can tell others how happy they were with their decision.

4. *Authority.* Any respected third party that speaks highly or positively about your product or service makes it easier for someone to buy from you. An authoritative voice is often the decisive factor. Publications, magazines, and news stories mentioning your product or service build credibility. People who are known for their expertise or knowledge and who use your product or service build your credibility. Symbols of affluence and authority, such as your dress, briefcase, wristwatch, and even the quality of the pen you use, increase your credibility, too. They imply that you are successful at selling a desirable and attractive product, especially at your prices.

5. *The Product or Service.* When your product provides the specific benefits that your customer is seeking, it has more credibility. When you show that the value the customer receives far outweighs the price, you build credibility and buying desire. When you back your product with guarantees and assurances, you increase the credibility you need to get the customer to make a buying decision.

The most successful salespeople are those who work continually to build their credibility in these five areas and with their customers.

ACTION EXERCISES

1. List three things that you can do to lower the fear of failure in the mind of your prospect.

2. List three key elements of megacredibility that you can incorporate into your sales activities.

SIXTEEN

Handle Objections Effectively

OBJECTIONS ARE a normal, natural, and unavoidable part of the sales process. Nonetheless, many salespeople become discouraged and disheartened when the customer begins to object to their offering on the basis of high price, better offers from competitors, and other reasons.

The fact is that customers today are bombarded by hundreds and even thousands of commercial messages. As a result, they are skeptical, suspicious, and careful with their time and money.

No matter what you are selling, customers will have questions and concerns that you must resolve before you can proceed to a sale. Your ability to handle these objections and concerns is a key skill that is essential to your sales success.

The best news is that objections are *good*. They indicate interest in your product or service. Objections often indicate that you have touched an emotional nerve and that you have connected with the prospect in some way. It turns out that successful sales have twice as many objections as unsuccessful sales do.

The Law of Six

The Law of Six is one of the most powerful principles you can use for identifying and overcoming objections. This law says that the number of objections to your product or service, whatever it is, is limited to no more than six.

Determine your six major objections. Ask yourself this question: "We could sell to everyone we talked to if our prospects just didn't say . . ."

Make a list of all the objections you get in a week or a month, and then divide them into six logical categories. They will differ from product to product and from market to market.

Once you have determined your six major objections, your job is to develop bulletproof answers to each of these common objections.

The Key Question

The key question in answering objections is, "Why don't our prospects buy our product from us?" Your job is to identify the answer to that question and then counter with a logical reason that eliminates the objection in the customer's mind.

Treat an objection as a *request* for more information. For example, the prospect says, "Your price is too high."

You respond by saying, "That's a good *question*. Why does our price seem to be higher than our competitors for this item? Let me see if I can answer that for you."

Compliment the objection. Encourage further objections. Say, "That's a good question! Let me see if I can answer it for you."

Make It Easy to Object

Each prospect has key objections or concerns that you must get out on the table. If the customer has a single objection lurking in the back of his mind, he may not say anything, but he will not buy, either. For this reason, no matter what the customer says, and no matter how often you may have heard it, you should hear out the objection completely.

Whenever the customer objects or makes a negative comment about your product, you should counter with your excellent listening skills. Remember to listen attentively, without interrupting; pause before replying; question for clarification; and, finally, feed it back in your own words, to make sure that you understand what the customer is saying.

Responding to Objections

There are several responses that you can use to reply to any objection. Remember, *the person who asks questions has control.* Always try to answer an objection with a question rather than an answer.

You can say, "Obviously you have a good reason for saying that; do you mind if I ask what it is?" And then just remain silent. Very often, the prospect does not have a good reason, and this will be revealed in the silence after your question.

Another way to respond to an objection is to ask, "How do you mean?" Or, "How do you mean, exactly?" And then remain silent.

Always use objections as an opportunity to build trust by listening intently to the other person's answer. The more intensely you listen to the prospect, the more the prospect likes you and trusts you and is open to purchasing your product or service.

Fighting Fuzzy Understanding

Most objections arise from fuzzy understanding. The problem your product will solve is not clear to the prospect. The need that your product will satisfy is not clear to the prospect. The benefits of your product or service to the prospect, relative to the price, are not clear. The unique selling proposition of your product or service is not clear.

And, finally, there is no urgency for the prospect to take action, or she sees no reason to act now rather than at some other time. These are all elements that contribute to the "fuzzy understanding" that leads to the customer saying, "Let me think it over."

Dealing with Price Objections

There are several proven ways for you to deal with price objections, which come up in almost every sale. When the prospect says, "Your price is too high," you respond by asking:

    a. Why do you say that?

    b. Why do you feel that way?

    c. Is price your only concern?

    d. How far apart are we?

If the prospect insists on knowing your price before you have identified his needs and have presented your benefits, delay the price conversation by saying, "I know price is important to you; may I come back to that in a minute?"

Remember, objections are the rungs on the ladder to sales success. The more objections you get, the more interested the prospect is in your product or service. When you hear an objection, you should be thankful and then begin turning the objection into reasons for buying.

ACTION EXERCISES

1. Identify the two or three most common objections that you receive from a qualified prospect for buying your product or service.

2. Identify the two or three best responses that you can give to your most common objections that enable you to go on and make the sale.

SEVENTEEN

Ask the Customer to Take Action

WHEN YOU HAVE reached the final stage of the sales conversation, and you are clear that the customer wants your product, needs your product, can use your product, and can afford your product, it is time to ask the prospect to take action.

When the prospect has indicated that he or she trusts you and believes in you, and expresses a desire to own or use your product or service, you can complete the transaction by using one of the following closing techniques.

Ask Confirming Questions

Before you close the sale, there are two confirming questions you can ask to be sure that the customer is ready for you to ask the closing question. The first is, "Do you have any questions or concerns that I haven't covered?" If the prospect says "no," the prospect is ready to buy.

A second question you can ask is, "Does this make sense to you so far?" If the prospect says "yes," the prospect is ready to make a buying decision.

Five Closing Questions

There are five key closing techniques that account for most of the high-level sales made by high-earning sales professionals. Here they are:

1. *The Preference Close.* Give the customer a choice between something and something else. Simply ask, "Which of these—A or B—do you prefer?"

It is much easier for a prospect to choose between a set of options than to give you a simple yes or no answer. Even if you are offering a single product, you can give the prospect a choice of payment terms, methods of delivery, or specific features that your product offers.

For example, you can ask, "Would you like to pay in cash, or would you like to finance it over twelve months?"

2. *The Invitational Close.* This is considered by many to be the most powerful closing technique of all. At the end of the sales conversation, when it is clear that the prospect likes what you have shown him or her, you simply ask, "Why don't you give it a try?"

Even if you are selling expensive or large items, you can close the sale by saying, "If you like it, why don't you give it a try?"

"Would you like to take it with you?"

"Would you like us to get started on this right away?"

"Is this what you had in mind?"

Always issue an invitation at the end of your sales presentation. Ask the person to make a buying decision.

3. *The Directive Close.* In this close, which is often called "the assumption close," you simply assume that the person has decided to buy and say, "If you have no further questions, then the next step is . . ."

For example, start off by saying, "Mr. Prospect, do you like what I have shown you so far?"

The prospect says, "Yes, it looks pretty good."

You say, "Well, then, the next step is . . ."

You then go on to describe the plan of action—what the customer does next to acquire your product and begin using and enjoying it: "Well, then, the next step is that we fill out this paperwork, I get a deposit from you in this particular amount, and we will begin producing this order and get it out to you by Wednesday of the week after next. How does that sound?"

4. *The Authorization Close.* You have reached the end of the sales conversation. The customer apparently likes the product or service that you have presented. You simply say, "Well, if you will just authorize this order, we'll get started right away."

You then take your order form, put a tick mark at the signature line, and pass the order form over to the customer to sign.

You say, "And I'll take care of all the details."

You tell the customer, "I will fill in all this information based on our discussion. I'll get the additional payment from your assistant, and we'll get this out to you next week."

5. *The Secondary Close.* This is very simple and quite powerful. It is often called "the minor point close," because you close on a minor point rather than a major point.

For example, you may be selling an expensive home. You ask a secondary question, the acceptance of which means that the customer has decided to buy. For example, you could ask, "Would you like to take occupancy on the first or the fifteenth of the month?"

Whichever option they choose, they've decided to buy the house. The occupancy date is a secondary issue. The choice or decision to buy the house is the major issue.

By the way, this is not an attempt to manipulate or mislead a prospect. It is a way of lowering the stress of making a large buying decision by giving the prospect something smaller to focus on.

If you were selling an expensive automobile, you could say, "Would you like the Michelin racing tires, or would you be happy with the factory tires?"

When the prospect says, "Well, I would like the Michelin racing tires," he has decided to buy the car.

The Most Powerful Word in Selling

The most important word in closing the sale is the word *ask*.

Ask the customer to make a buying decision. Ask the customer if you can proceed to the next stage of the sale. At the very least, ask: "What would you like to do now?"

The most important quality in developing the skill set of closing sales is *courage.* You develop courage through practice.

At the very least, at the end of your sales conversation, if it is not possible or appropriate for you to close the sale and get the order, agree to the next stage. "What should we do now?" Set a date for the next meeting where you can present more information and speak with additional people to keep the sales conversation moving forward.

ACTION EXERCISES

1. What must you be sure to do before asking the customer to make a buying decision?

2. Design, practice, and perfect one closing question that you can use most of the time in your sales activities.

EIGHTEEN

Provide Excellent Customer Service

PETER DRUCKER wrote that "the purpose of a business is to create and keep a customer."

How can you tell if the business is fulfilling its purpose in a satisfactory way? Simple. Customer satisfaction. The true measure of business success is that your customers are happy with their decision to buy from you, and are internally motivated to buy from you again.

The very best people and the best companies are obsessed with customer service. The customer is the most important single person in their thinking. Everything they do is organized to satisfy their customers better in some way.

Sam Walton once said, "We only have one boss, and that is the customer. And he can fire us at any time by simply deciding to spend his money somewhere else."

Maintain Service Excellence

Your ability to develop and maintain a reputation for high levels of service excellence is the key to the growth and prosperity of your company and to success in your career.

The success of your business in the future will be determined by your quality ranking in your marketplace today. According to studies done at Harvard, the customer's definition of quality includes both the product or service you sell, plus the way that it is sold and delivered.

Question: What is your quality ranking? On a scale of one to ten, how do you rank with your competitors in terms of the quality of your product *and* the quality of the way that it is sold, delivered, and serviced?

Four Levels of Service

There are four levels of customer service for any company:

1. *Satisfy your customers.* A customer who is satisfied with the product or service that you have sold and delivered is the minimum requirement for survival. But if all you do is satisfy your customers, your customers will be open to competitive offers, have minimum loyalty, and will seldom recommend you to others.

2. *Exceed customer expectations.* This is when you do something more than your customer expected and more than your competitors do, to differentiate yourself from them. Your ability to exceed customer expectations is the minimum requirement for the growth of your business. And

remember, whatever you do to exceed customer expectations today will soon be copied by your competitor tomorrow.

3. *Delight your customers.* This is when you start to move into the arena of the fast-growth companies in your industry. You do something that not only exceeds expectations, but actually delights and brings a smile of happiness to the face of your customers.

A very successful high-class restaurant chain has its waiters come around to your table after the meal and offer a free after-dinner drink or a glass of port wine. This offer is both unexpected and generous. The last impression that people have as they leave that restaurant is one of customer service excellence. And they return again and again.

Often, after a sale, a senior executive of the company will phone to thank the customer personally for choosing to do business with the firm. This is another simple way of delighting your customers and setting them up emotionally to buy from you again and again.

4. *Amaze your customers.* This is when you do something that is completely beyond expectations and even beyond just delighting your customers. You actually amaze them in such a way that they tell others and talk about you to their friends.

Some years ago, the Denver branch of FedEx, whose promise is, "When you absolutely, positively have to have it overnight," experienced a blizzard that closed the major roads leading out of Denver and made it impossible for FedEx trucks to deliver their letters and packages. They then did something remarkable.

Individual Initiative

Because the blizzard had closed the mountain passes, the station manager chartered a helicopter at a cost of about $8,000 to fly over the snowbound highways and deliver the FedEx packages to customers in Colorado Springs, landing in the parking lot of a major shopping center.

This was such an amazing demonstration of FedEx's commitment to fulfilling its promise to its customers that the story was picked up by all the newspapers and featured on national radio and television. To this day, customers in Colorado still talk about the "grand gesture" of chartering a helicopter to deliver packages overnight.

Follow Up After the Sale

As a salesperson, you can exceed expectations and both amaze and delight your prospects by the way you follow up after the sale.

There are four keys to an effective follow-up:

1. Once you have taken the order, process the paperwork and get things moving quickly.

2. Keep the prospect informed. If there is any delay or problem at all, immediately contact the customer so that the person knows what is going on. Customers are understanding and accommodating, as long as you let them know. Practice the "no surprises" principle.

3. Send a thank-you card, note, or e-mail immediately after the sale. If it is a big enough sale, send a present of some kind, even if it's only flowers, a box of chocolates, or—my favorite—a gift basket from a local company. This gesture is a powerful way to encourage repeat business.

4. Make sure that the last contact customers have with you is always positive. The last contact leaves the deepest impression. This is the one they remember the most. When you take the order, take the time to thank customers for buying your product or service from you and assure them that they will be happy with their purchase and that you will do everything possible to ensure this happiness. Tell your customers to call you at any time if they have any questions or concerns, and give them your private cell phone number. These are the kind of final impressions that amaze and delight your customers and cause them to come back and buy from you again and again.

ACTION EXERCISES

1. Decide upon one action that you can take to delight your customers during and after every sale in the future.

2. Decide upon one action that you are going to take consistently to make the customer's buying experience even happier than it is today.

NINETEEN

Keep Customers for Life

A DIRECT SALE to a commercial customer today costs more than $400 in terms of time, travel, advertising, lead generation, and other expenses. Acquiring a customer at this cost can put a company out of business unless that customer buys again and again.

The best salespeople and the best companies implement strategies to acquire customers and to keep them for life. Your goal must be to develop long-term customer relationships and then hold on to them in the face of ever more aggressive competition.

When you install a customer acquisition and retention strategy, you do more to build and maintain long-term customer relationships than ever before. By continually thinking in terms of "customers for life," your success in sales will be assured.

Focus on the Second Sale

The first sale with any customer is always the hardest and most expensive. You can get the first sale with discounts, deceit, or bonus offers. But it is the second sale that is the most important. The second sale is the proof that you have delivered on the promises you made during the first sale.

In reality, you actually go out each day and you sell your promises to people in exchange for their money. You promise that your product or service will give them certain benefits that they are not currently enjoying. When they come back and buy from you again, they are putting their stamp of approval on your offerings and confirming that you did deliver on your promises.

Resales and Referrals Are Almost Free

Resales to satisfied customers are ten times easier than new sales to new customers. A resale only requires one-tenth of the time and effort to achieve. This is why most successful companies measure their success by how often their customers buy again.

A referral from a satisfied customer is fifteen times easier to sell to than a cold call. Selling to a referral requires only one-fifteenth of the time, cost, and effort to make. In fact, if you have a good referral, the sale is 90 percent made before you walk in the door.

Create a Golden Chain

Once you have made the sale and the customer is happy, develop a "golden chain of referrals" by asking everyone to refer you to other interested prospects. Ask confidently. Ask expectantly. Ask courteously. But always ask customers and even noncustomers if they can refer someone else to you.

When asking people for a referral, assure them that you will put no pressure on the person whose name they are providing. People are hesitant about sharing referrals until they are convinced that the friend or associate that they are referring will not be unhappy or angry with them for giving you their name.

Generate Word-of-Mouth Advertising

The most powerful method for you to generate referrals in today's competitive marketplace is by triggering *word-of-mouth* on the part of your happy customers. Your aim is to make your customers part of your sales force by getting them to actually sell for you when they talk to other prospective customers. The way that you motivate your customers to sell for you is by giving them outstanding customer service.

The most important element of outstanding customer service is always speed. Speedy response to questions, concerns, and inquiries is a key measure of how many referrals you are likely to get. Fast action on complaints is vital. Regular follow-up and continuous customer care are essential tools for getting referrals.

Practice *the golden rule of selling*: Serve your customers the way you would like your suppliers to serve you if you were a customer. Serve your customers the way you would serve your spouse, your mother, or your closest friend. Go the extra mile. Always do more than is expected.

The Ultimate Question

Fred Reichheld of Bain & Company studied the elements of excellent customer service for many years before finally concluding that there was one single question that was more indicative of customer satisfaction and referral business than any other single question.

He called it the ultimate question: "Based on your experience with us, would you recommend us to others?"

The willingness of a customer to recommend you to others is the highest level of customer satisfaction. Very often, if you form a good relationship with noncustomers, they will like and trust you so much that they will recommend you to others even if they do not buy themselves.

Always Ask

At the end of the sales conversation, you can ask this question: "On a scale of one to ten, would you recommend us to others?"

Of course, your goal is to get a ten. This means that this customer will become a "raving fan." He will become a customer advocate. He will tell all of his friends to buy from you as well.

But what if you receive a grade of less than ten—say, a seven or eight? You say, "Thank you for your answer," then immediately ask, "What would we have to do to earn a ten from you next time?"

Keep asking your customers, "How are we doing?" and "How could we do better next time?" The highest-paid and most successful salespeople are those who develop a book of business—a series of satisfied customers who buy from them again and again, provide faster and easier sales, are less price sensitive, and form the basis for the growth of any business. This is your goal as well.

Your Customer Service Strategy

Develop a customer sales and service strategy that enables you to get and keep customers for life.

This customer service approach does not happen by accident. It requires careful planning, discussion, and training of everyone who deals with your customers. All successful salespeople and businesses are known for how well they treat their customers. This must be your goal always.

ACTION EXERCISES

1. What one action can you take with every customer and prospective customer that will cause them to want to refer other prospects to you?

2. Determine one action or behavior on the part of anyone in your company that might reduce customer satisfaction and referral business. How could you eliminate it, and how fast?

TWENTY

Manage Your Time Effectively

MORE THAN 100 years of research and countless millions of dollars have been invested in seeking the causes for success and failure in selling. At last, we have the answers. They are simply this: People are highly paid because they spend more of their time doing things of higher value. People are underpaid because they spend more of their time doing things of lower value.

Salespeople who spend every minute of every day focusing on high-value activities eventually rise to the top of their fields and make both a lot of sales and a lot of money.

Salespeople who waste their time in low-value activities seldom accomplish anything of importance—even if they represent the best companies with the best products in the best markets.

Practice the Pareto Principle

The Pareto principle is the most important time management concept in the field of professional selling.

This principle says that 80 percent of the value of what you do comes from 20 percent of your activities. This 80/20 rule applies to all aspects of selling and to all activities. Apply this rule to your prospects, your customers, and your products.

Divide your customers and prospects by value, with the A-list being high-value prospects/customers who can represent 80 percent of your sales. B-list customers are medium-value customers and prospects, and the C-list would be low-value customers and prospects.

Practice "creative procrastination" on the 80 percent of your tasks that only represent 20 percent of the value of what you do. Creative procrastination is what you use when you consciously and deliberately decide *not* to do certain things that are of low value so that you can focus your attention on those activities of high value.

Your Job Description

The job description of a salesperson is the same as the purpose of a business. Your job is to *create and keep customers.*

Spend 80 percent of your time creating customers and only 20 percent of your time keeping customers. Always be asking, "Where is my next sale coming from?" Whatever your answer to that question, be sure that it's what you are working on virtually every minute of every day.

Therefore, spend 80 percent of your time prospecting and presenting. Spend only 20 percent of your time following up and closing. Don't mix them up. Keep your focus on prospecting and presenting.

Get Better at What You Do

One of the most powerful ways to increase your income consistently is to get better at the most important things you do—at prospecting, presenting, and following up and closing. Every investment in self-improvement, whether it be in books, audiotapes, videos, or seminars, gives you a payoff ten times, twenty times, and even fifty times the amount that it costs to learn the new ideas in the first place. Many salespeople have gone from the bottom to the top, from rags to riches, as the result of one single sales seminar or even one sales idea that was ideal for them, their product, their market, and their customers at that time.

The Minutes Principle

To double your sales, implement the "minutes principle" into your sales activities. This rule says that you are making all the sales you are making today with the number of minutes you are spending face-to-face with prospects and customers.

When you increase the number of minutes you are spending face-to-face with customers, by the law of averages, you will increase your sales and income by that percentage.

Here is how you use this principle: Get a stopwatch to measure your current level of sales activities. Each time you go in to see a customer, click it on, and when you come out, click it off. The stopwatch will accumulate the number of minutes that you spend with customers each day. Write that number down so that you are clear about it.

Improve Your Score

Resolve to increase the number of minutes you spend face-to-face with customers by 10 percent per week. If you are currently spending ninety minutes per day, the general average, and you increase that by 10 percent, you will be spending nine more minutes per week with customers. You will immediately see an increase in your sales and your income.

Keep improving by 10 percent per week until you are spending twice as much time—fully 180 minutes on average—in face-to-face interactions with customers. Almost without exception, by doubling your minutes of face time, you will double your income, and sometimes far faster than you can imagine.

Work All the Time You Work

From the time you start early in the morning until the time you quit, late in the day, resolve to work all the time you work. Don't waste time. Don't play with your e-mail or chat with your coworkers. Don't allow yourself to be distracted by electronic interruptions such as phone calls, messages, and voice mail. Work all the time you work. This decision alone will make you one of the most successful salespeople in your field in a very short time.

ACTION EXERCISES

1. Select one time management activity that can help you to increase your productivity, and begin practicing it every day for the following month until it becomes a habit.

2. Select one time-wasting activity, and resolve to eliminate it for one month, until that becomes a habit as well.

TWENTY-ONE

There Are No Limits!

YOU HAVE THE SKILLS and the ability right now to sell and earn *twice* as much as you are earning today, and probably much, much more. It has been said that "your attitude, more than your aptitude, determines your altitude."

If you want to become physically fit, you engage in physical exercise each day. If you want to become mentally fit, you engage in certain mental exercises each day as well. There are seven things you can do to motivate yourself and to keep yourself performing at your best all day long. Here they are.

Be the Best

Make a decision to become excellent in the field of selling. Resolve to pay any price, make any sacrifice, invest any amount of time necessary, for as long as it takes, to get into the top 10 percent or 20 percent of income earners in your field.

The main reason that people don't get into the top 10 percent in selling is because they never make a decision to do it. They think about it and dream about it and wish that they were up there earning the big money, but they never make a do-or-die decision that they are going to pay whatever price is necessary to excel in the field of selling.

The good news is that all sales skills are learnable. You can learn any skill you need to learn to achieve any sales goals you can set for yourself. There are no limits.

Learn the Key Skill

Identify your limiting skill to greater success in selling. Imagine you could wave a magic wand and, overnight, become absolutely excellent in any one skill in the field of selling. What one skill, if you were absolutely excellent at it, would help you the most to increase your sales and income?

The fact is that you could be only one skill away from doubling your income and becoming one of the highest-paid people in your industry. And when you answer this question, you'll probably know what that skill might be.

Get Around Winners

Associate with positive people most of the time. Your choice of the people that you associate with at work, after work, and during evenings and weekends will have an enormous impact on your impact, your personality, and your level of achievement.

Preserve Your Health and Energy

Take excellent care of your physical health. People live longer and live better today than at any other time in human history. And most of what you do with your health is entirely under your control.

Improve Your Mental Pictures

Practice positive visualization: See yourself as the very best in your field. Remember that the person you see on the inside is the person you will eventually be on the outside. All improvement in your results on the outside begins with an improvement in your mental pictures on the inside. When you visualize yourself as confident, positive, and absolutely excellent in your field, your thoughts, words, feelings, and actions will express that mental picture in everything you do.

Speak Positively to Yourself

Talk to yourself positively. Control your inner dialogue. Fully 95 percent of your emotions are determined by the way you talk to yourself as you go through your day. Positive, happy people talk to themselves in a positive and constructive way.

Take Continuous Action

Become intensely action-oriented in everything you do. As Einstein said, "Nothing happens until something moves."

Well, in sales, nothing happens until you move as well. Start earlier. Work harder. Stay longer.

Get going. Get busy. Move fast. Increase your speed and rate of activity.

Remember, the faster you move, the more people you see. The more people you see, the more sales you will make. The more sales you make, the more income you will earn. The more income you earn, the more motivated you will be to see even more people, make more sales, and earn even higher income.

When you begin practicing these ideas, hour by hour, day in and day out, nonstop, relentlessly, your sales will go up and up and up. Within a few months or even a few weeks, you will become one of the most successful and highest-paid people in your field. And I hope you do.

There are no limits!

ACTION EXERCISES

1. Resolve today to engage in one continuous activity that will make you excellent in your chosen field of sales.

2. Practice one activity, such as visualization, affirmation, or continuous action, that will help you stay positive and motivated throughout the selling day.